Trees Believe

POEMS

Natacha Warwick

ILLUSTRATED BY: SHANNEN MARIE PARADERO

www.trafford.com

North America & international
toll-free: 1 888 232 4444 (USA & Canada)
fax: 812 355 4082

CONTENTS

DEDICATION

I BELIEVE IN THE POWER OF THE HOLY SPIRIT, I BELIEVE IN GOD, AND JESUS CHRIST OUR LORD AND SAVIOUR.

JESUS I LOVE YOU, THANK YOU FOR LOVING US.
THANK YOU FOR SEVILLE, SHE IS SO AMAZING, I LOVE MY LITTLE DOGGY.

DEAR REVEREND JESSICA SCHAAP, I APPRECIATE YOUR HEART, YOU LOVE JESUS SO MUCH, THANK YOU FOR YOUR TIME AND UNDERSTANDING. MANY BLESSINGS TO YOU!

DEAR REVEREND STEPHANIE SHEPARD, YOU ARE A BEAUTIFUL ROSE, TO BE CHERISHED FOREVER, THANK YOU FOR YOUR THOUGHTFUL WAYS, YOUR LAUGHTER AND YOUR HEART. JESUS LOVES YOU!

DEAR ARCHBISHOP MELISSA SKELTON, THANK YOU FOR BEING A GUIDING LIGHT TO ALL OF THE DIOCESE OF NEW WESTMINSTER. WE LOVE YOU, YOUR HEART AND YOUR MESSAGES OF FAITHFULNESS TO GOD.

THANK YOU TO THE TRAFFORD TEAM FOR HELPING ME WITH MY WORK OF ART. GREAT JOB!!!

I WANT TO THANK HEATHER SCHAMEHORN FOR TAKING CARE OF SEVILLE EACH DAY, SEVILLE AND I LOVE YOU SO MUCH. WE REALLY APPRECIATE ALL OF YOUR HEART AND SOUL. I KNOW GOD APPRECIATES YOUR KINDNESS AND THE SHARING OF YOUR TIME. SEVILLE IS SO LUCKY TO HAVE YOU IN HER LIFE.

DEAR PAUL, YOU ARE SUCH A GOOD FRIEND.
I KNOW TWO PAUL'S, BOTH ARE AMAZING. THE BEST A FRIEND CAN GET, SUPPORTIVE, SHARING AND CARING. KINDA LIKE PAUL FROM THE BIBLE, HE KNOWS THE TRUTH, AND LIVES IT.

GRANDMA BE, YOU ARE FULL OF LIFE, AND YOU ARE FUNNY. YOU ARE ONE OF MY FAV'S, STAY STRONG. THANK YOU EAST COAST FAMILY FOR YOUR BRILLIANCE, LOVE AND WONDERFUL WAYS.

MY WEST COAST FAMILY IS AMAZING AS WELL. LOTS OF LOVE TO YOUR HEARTS!

I LOVE YOU ANGELS!

I ALSO LOVE THE PARISHIONERS AT MY CHURCH, THANK YOU.

JOSE, YOU ARE AN AMAZING HUMAN. YOU ARE A TRUE FRIEND, AND WE APPRECIATE YOU. TAKE CARE OF YOURSELF, SEVILLE AND I LOVE YOU.

THANKS MOM.

JESUS, FOR YOU REIGN, IN THE GLORY OF THE POWER THAT IS LOVE.

FOREVER AND EVER,

AMEN.

TREES BELIEVE

COLOUR ME SOFTLY
WITH A LIGHT TOUCH
I'M GREEN, I BELIEVE, I LIVE VERY MUCH
RAIN DROPS LIKE PETALS
LIGHT INTO THE WIND
GLORY TO THE HIGHEST AND SO WE BEGIN
AS I BELIEVE I SWAY AND LET THE LIGHT IN

AUGUST 15, 2016

TREES

GREEN LIGHT

RISE ABOVE

INFUSE ME

I'M IN LOVE

THE ROOTS ARE IN

BRING ME

I BEGIN

TO SEE

THE LIGHT

INFINITE DREAMS

TONIGHT

A SHADE OF GREEN

MAGNIFY MY LOVE

I LOVE THE WAY

YOU LOOK

STANDING TALL

SPREAD YOUR WINGS

IT'S OKAY TO

FALL

IN LOVE

WITH ME

TREES

BELIEVE

MARCH 3, 2016 11:34 P.M.

TREE AURA

AS I LOOK AT YOU
I SEE ALL THE COLOURS
A BEAUTIFUL CASCADE
OF LIGHT
THAT SHINES
SO
BRIGHT
ENERGY FILLED
ICING
ENERGY
BOUNDLESS LOVE
FROM ABOVE
TREES
BELIEVE

AUGUST 30, 2015 10:00 P.M.

FERN

FRONDS

GREEN HUE

PARADING LIGHT

UNFURL

FLOWING GATE

SPREAD

MAKE UP

WATER ME

SOIL

SUNSHINE

WHISKERS

CHLOROPHYLL

PRIDE

VASCULAR

TISSUE

STEM

CELL

FIDDLEHEAD

VIOLIN

MOONLIGHT

SONATA

ANCIENT

2017

SOIL

I GIVE LIFE
TO YOU
DEAR FLOWERS
MY HEART BELONGS TO YOU
AS YOU BREATHE, THE
RHYTHM OF YOUR
LIFE INTERTWINES WITH MINE
LIGHT INFUSES US
MY SOUL DOES BLEED,
WATER, LIGHT
HARMONY

LET ME NOURISH YOUR PETALS,
YOUR ROOTS TELL ME
WHY I'M HERE
TO BE CLOSE TO YOU
MY DEAR
LIGHT US UP
WATER ME DOWN
I'M FULL OF YOUR WONDER
COLOUR ME BRIGHT
I'LL BREATHE YOU IN

MARCH 28, 2017

TREE PRAYER

LIGHT US UP ONE BY ONE
TELL THE MOON AND THE
SUN TO COME CLOSE

HEAVEN'S EQUATOR,
SATURN'S RINGS
KARMA DECLARED HEAVEN SINGS
AS I BELIEVE I SWAY AND
LET THE LIGHT IN
GLORY TO THE HIGHEST,
SO LET US BEGIN
THE PRIEST DOES HER
HAND DANCE,
THE SERMON IS SUNG, GOD
WATCHES US, ONE
BY ONE

I FEEL THE WIND, DON'T
YOU, HERE IT
COMES ACHOO
MY BRANCHES ARE
HUNG JUST RIGHT,
EVERY YEAR I GROW,
COUNT MY RINGS
HALO
THE RAIN IT FALLS, STARTING IN
SEPTEMBER, I FEEL A
CHILL, DOWN MY
SPINE IN NOVEMBER, THE WIND IT
CLIMBS, MY ROOTS
KNOW, IT'S TIME TO
TURN IN, IT'S SNOW.

BRANCHES ARE THERE
LIKE THE WIND,
SOMETIMES WE SWIM,
IT'S ALL UP TO HIM.

AS I BELIEVE I SWAY AND
LET THE LIGHT IN

APRIL 5, 2017 1:35 P.M.

TREES

THE FINEST FILAMENT	YOUR
THE GRANDEST FIR	OWN
PARDON ME	RAIN
I CONCUR	TALL
THE FAINTEST LIGHT	SPRUCE
THE WILDEST GAIT	FALL
STANDING STRAIGHT	JUNIPER
	FOXTAIL PINE
PINE	
CONE	XYLEM
	PHLOEM
THE THRONE	
YOUR MAJESTY	TO BE
	IS KNOWN

2017

Trees Believe

There was a   Time   An old growth   tree   fell down sudden   ly.   It

shook the Earth.   He   set it free.   God rose   Tri - um - phant -   ly.

Trees   Be - lieve.

CHERRY BLOSSOMS

SO BEAUTIFUL

WHY WEEP

I PICK UP YOUR PETALS

WHY DO YOU CRY

YOUR PINK HUES

ARE SO LOVELY

WOULD YOU PICK ME

FROM THE GROUND

THE SOFTNESS OF YOUR LIPS

ARE ONLY DEFINED

BY THE ACCENT OF

YOUR LIGHT

I AM DEFINED BY PETALS

YOU ARE MY ONLY

BE ONE WITH ME

BE MINE, TOGETHER

IN TUNE WITH THE

RHYTHMS

IN LOVE WITH HUES OF WHITE

BE ONE WITH THE LIGHT

MY BLOSSOMS

YOUR BOSOM

IN LOVE TONIGHT

THE SEA SCREAMS IN DELIGHT

WE KISS GOOD NIGHT.

SPRING 2015

THREE CHERRY BLOSSOM HAIKUS

IRIDESCENT PINK
VELVET UNDERTONES, PINK HUES
BLOOM, I NEED SOME ROOM

MARCH 23, 2017

BLOWING IN THE BREEZE
THE WAY I FEEL ABOUT SPRING
BLOSSOMS UNDERFOOT

MARCH 24, 2017

PINK DUST, CHERRY BREATH
THE WAY THEY FALL INTO YOU
RAIN DANCE, BLOSSOMING

APRIL 5, 2017

CHERRY BLOSSOM BOOGIE

PINK DUST

CHERRY BREATH

RAIN DANCE

PETALS EVERYWHERE

PINK SHINE

TREE TALL

THE WAY THEY FALL

APRIL 5, 2017 2:30 P.M.

DRUNK ON A ROSE

DRUNK ON A ROSE, MY HEART IS TOTALLY THERE,
WHEN I THINK OF YOU, I ONLY CAN STARE.
BLEEDING ROSE, WE ARE ONLY APART, TAKE MY HAND,
IT'S A START.

2018

ROSE ME

SIMPLICITY

MAGNIFY

CURLS

ENVELOPE ME

TWIRLS

OCTOBER 1, 2016 2:30 P.M.

ROSE GARDEN

DELIGHT

SMELLING SYMPHONY

UPTIGHT

TCHAIKOVSKY

BACH

VIOLIN

CHOPIN

COMPOSER'S

CHAIR

I STAND UNAWARE

CELLO

AND BRASS

PIERCE

BOMB BLAST

TUNING FORK

ELEPHANT

STORK

STRING QUARTET

BEETHOVEN

WAS DEAF

1826

OPUS 131

STRAVINSKY'S

SON

DOSTOYEVSKY

RUSSIAN

2018

PETALS EMBRACE

PETALS EMBRACE
SEE THE LOOK ON MY FACE
THE SKY'S ONLY TRACE
SNOW COMES IN TIME
NOVEMBER A RHYME

LEAVES ON THE GROUND
BRANCHES ASTOUND

FLOWERS ASKEW
DUST TO RENEW

WINTER IS HERE
WHITENESS APPEARS
DEW DISAPPEARS
FROSTY MIRRORS

THE DANCE OF SNOWFLAKES
WINTER ROMANCE
CANDLES LIT
CHRISTMAS
UNITES
THE
LIGHT

2017

23

LIGHT PINK

SOFTNESS

LUXURIOUS

PETALS

PAPER THIN

DELICATE

SCENT

STEMMED

PERPETUAL

WEIGHTLESS

TWIRLS

2017

CANADA

HAVE YOU SEEN THE MOUNTAINS
HAVE YOU SEEN OUR HEARTS
DON'T PASS US BY ON YOUR DOG
SLED ARCTIC ADVENTURE

WE LIVE BY THE SEA, THE
RIVERS AND THE LAKES
WE LIKE TO SKATE, ENJOY
ARTWORK AND FINE WINE
SOME EVEN SAY WE ARE
CLOSER TO THE DIVINE

WE STAND LIKE AN ARMY
TAKEN EVERY LAST BREATH,
AS A TRUE CANADIAN I AM
ONE WITH THE REST.
SOME SPEAK FRENCH,
OTHER'S MANDARIN
I SPEAK CANADIAN
TRUE ON MY KNEES.

I AM DEVOTED TO MY COUNTRY,
DEVOTED TO THE LAND,
LET US THANK EACH OTHER, AND
REMEMBER THAT WE STAND,
UNITED ON ALL FRONTS,
DRIVEN TO BE GREAT.
LOVE ONE ANOTHER, IT IS
IMPORTANT THAT WE STATE,
I LOVE YOU IN MY HEART,
UNTIL THE END OF TIME.

BE THANKFUL AND BE KIND.

CANADA IS SUPREME, REMEMBER
TO LOVE YOUR LEADER,
AND GOD MOST OF ALL.

2016

RAIN FLIGHTS

RAIN FLIGHTS
DOWNPOUR
I'M IN TEARS
I LOVE YOU MORE
JESUS CHRIST
IS ALWAYS HERE
AS IT RAINS
I HEAR
THE WHISPERS
OF LIGHT
HITS SO HARD
I SWEAR
IT MUST BE
TEARS
FROM
UP
HERE

2017

GLOVES

HIDDEN, METALLIC,
WATCH ME GLOW
I GLIDE LIKE THE RIVER
UNDER THE SNOW

I'M HERE, YOU'RE THERE,
MOON WALK, WE SHINE
I DAZE, YOU SNOOZE,
SHE CAME LOOSE.

SNAP BACK, VELCRO STRAP
SMOOTH MOVES, ENTIRELY MINE
I'VE COME CLOSE TO THE DIVINE

STREET TALK, TREES
TALL, YOU ARE NOT
SMALL.
TOFINO BREEZE, STAY
ON YOUR KNEES.

THE RAINFOREST BREATHES.
KINDNESS FLOWS TO
HEAVEN, GREATNESS
BECOMES A PART OF ME.
LEVEL 5 ENTIRELY.

GOODNESS, TREAT ME, HEAVENLY.
JUST PUT THESE GLOVES ON.
I KNOW....I KNOW...

OCTOBER 28, 2015 9:52 P.M.

FLAT

FLAT

BEHOLD
THE
AMAZING
ONE OUNCE
TO SHINE
FOREVER, BE MINE
WE CAME, WE SAW
INSPIRED, WE FLAWED
ONE EARTH

IT'S ROUND
HEAVEN SENT

I FOUND, GOD
HORIZON
WE SPOKE
TOGETHER
ONE SPOKE
PYTHAGORAS

ARISTOTLE IT'S TRUE

DECEMBER 2, 2015 2:07 P.M.

SEA OTTER

OCEAN DEPTHS

KELP BATHS

PUP

WRAP ME UP

PAW TO PAW

BITE MY NOSE

WEBBED TOED

FLIPPER FEET

ALL FUR

ALL GROOMED

WILL ZOOM

MARINE MAMMAL

SUPER FLEXIBLE

SCULL WITH TAIL

NO NEED FOR A SAIL

LIE ON YOUR BACK

STOMACH SNACK

MUNCH ON YOUR FISH

BELLY DISH

CRAB CRUMBS

OPPOSABLE THUMBS

VIBRISSAE

DETECT PREY

APRIL 23, 2017

31

MOTHER

A MOTHER NURTURES
IS ALWAYS THERE
EVER CARING
KNOWING STARE
HOLDING YOU CLOSE
STANDING STRONG
A MOTHER NURTURES
IN THE LIGHT
HEAVEN BESTOWS
A LOVING HAND
BLESS YOUR MOM
A COMMAND
A HEART MESSENGER
LOVING YOU
A MOTHER
TO FIND YOU

MOTHER'S DAY 2018

DYING

IT IS SO HARD TO DO
THEN IT HAPPENS
THE BIG UNDUE
HOW'S MY HAIR
MY UNDERWEAR
NO ONE KNOWS
WHERE I WENT
IT'S UP TO YOU
I'M SPENT

DECEMBER 1, 2016

SEVILLE'S ORANGE YOU GONNA CLEAN ME TUNE

TUXEDO TIME

HOSE ME DOWN

I'M IN TOWN

SOAP SUDS

BATH TIME

SING ME A RHYME

HONEY I'M HOME

THROW ME A BONE

ALOHA

CLEAN MY PAW

EAR WIPE

HAIR BRUSH

I'M IN A RUSH

TICKLE MY ELBOW

WASH MY TOES

PLEASE CLEAN MY NOSE

LAVENDER

INFLORESCENCE

I AM PRESENT

JULY 3, 2015 1:24 P.M.

35

TUXEDO SEVILLE

TUXEDO SEVILLE

SQUISHY PANTS

PEANUT BUTTER AND JELLY

DAISY

STRETCH LIMO

BABY CAKES

BOSTON

TUX

QUEEN OF DIAMONDS

CRAZY FACE CHAMPION

BLACK THUNDER

CREATURE VILLE

SLEEPY HEAD

MOMMY'S BABY

PETTING ZOO

SQUISH MEISTER

PIKACHU

EASTER MONDAY, APRIL 17, 2017

A BIRTHDAY POEM FOR A QUEEN

SEA BREEZE

SEE MY CROWN

DON'T

LOOK DOWN

LOVE MY FACE

I'M ALSO AN ACE

HEAR MY SONG

FOOT LOOSE

FREEWAY

I AM THE WAY

LEARN FROM ME

WEAR A CROWN

WATCH THE STARS

I'M IN TOWN

DESTINY

INFINITY

I CAME TO SERVE

THIS IS WHAT WE DESERVE

LISTEN TO MY VOICE

YOU HAVE A CHOICE

2017

ELIZABETH

WHAT A THRONE

TO BE KNOWN

MAY I

MADAME.....

BE YOURS

NOW

MAY I WEAR YOUR CROWN

TO WEAR IT BEST, I AM ONE

THE TIDES TURN

TO THE WEST

SEE MY GRACE

IN THE DAY

HAVE YOUR WAY

YOU MAY STAY

TO SAY IT BEST

YOU ARE BETH

TO SAY I AM WAY

AHEAD OF THE DAY

APOLOGIZE

IS MY DEMISE

WE BEGIN

ANEW

TO EACH MAN

WE ARE FREE

IN LOVE WITH ME

SEE MY BREAST

IT IS FRESH

SEE MY DRESS

OUT OF THE WAY

I MAY SIT

BE ONE WITH IT

2015

TRUMP

BLURR
SHOULDERS
GIVE ME A MOMENT TO
SHARE MY VIEWS
DOWNTIME
DOWNTOWN
WEAR MY CROWN
GOLD, SO I'M TOLD, HAIR A'BLAZIN',
EXECUTIVES RAVIN'
LIKE MY TIE,
I'M THE GUY

TIGHT TWIST, TAKE A
LOOK AT MY WRIST.
VANCOUVER I'M HERE
SNL LET'S BEGIN

MY SMILE'S A MILE WIDE
I'VE GOT ZEROES TO BUY

PRESIDENTIAL CAMPAIGN
YOU'RE A PAIN
I CAN'T WAIT FOR IT TO BE OVER
SO I CAN REIGN

NOVEMBER 12, 2015 10:37 P.M.

ARC

WATER	CHOCOLATE
TEA	UN PETITE ASSIETTE
SYMPHONY	RENAISSANCE
JAZZ	OUVERT
SPLASHES	HONEYCOMB
ROMANTIC	SOMPTUOSITÉ
OVERTURES	BREAD
FANTASTIC	WINNER
HORS D'OEUVRES	BUTTERCREAM
	LIVING
	DREAM

2017

CHRISTMAS MAJESTY

I HEAR THE SOUND OF YOUR VOICE
SING ALLELUIA
I WATCHED YOU GROW
INTO A GREAT MAN
YOU ARE HEAVEN'S BLESSING
I PRAY WITH BOTH HANDS

I CAN HEAR YOUR HEART SONG
SING ALLELUIA
BREATHE INTO ME
AS EACH SNOW FALLS
I BARELY CAN SEE
YOU SAY THE BLIND WILL SEE
I KNOW THE TRUTH
IT'S YOU IN ME, AND ME IN YOU

LORD JESUS
MY LOVE ALIGHT
SACRED HEART
AFLIGHT

SING INTO MY HEART
SING ALLELUIA
PRAY FOR ME
SWEET MAJESTY
I LIVE FOR THEE
TRINITY
I BELIEVE
IT'S ME

FOR THOSE WHO RECOGNIZE THE LIGHT, FOR THOSE WHO
NEED A LIFT, AND FOR THOSE WHO WANT A BLESSING. AMEN

SEPTEMBER 21, 2016

PRAYER

I LOOK TO GOD
IN HIS HOLINESS
YOU SHINE SO BRIGHT
YOUR HIGHNESS
I PRAY TO YOU
ENLIGHTEN MY WAY
FIGHT THE DEVIL
THE ORIGINAL WAY
YOU PAID FOR OUR SINS
YOU PAID WITH YOUR BLOOD

I'M ON MY KNEES
HEAVEN'S TRUE LOVE
WE SHARE YOUR BREAD
AND DRINK YOUR WINE
ONLY YOU COULD DO THIS FOR
MANKIND

IN THE NAME OF JESUS

AMEN

JANUARY 19, 2017

REVEREND

TRUTH SEEKING   EXPERIENCED

DEFINING LIGHT   SUBLIME

CROSSED   ENDLESS

LISTENING   TIME

SHARING   HOLY

HEARTFELT   PARADIGM

LOVE   DEVOTED

INTERTWINED   BLESSED

WITH   HEAVEN'S DRESS

DIVINE

2018

PRAY FOR THE LIGHT POEM
CHRIST IS RISEN

LORD, WE KNOW YOU

HAVE ATONED

WE WAIT TO SEE YOUR THRONE

YOU HAVE GONE DOWN

TO THE DEEP

HELL HATH AWAKEN

THE LORD HATH TAKEN OUR SINS

COME, HOLY SPIRIT, COME

LORD, AS YOU RISE

MAKE SURE SATAN IS

KISSED GOODBYE

WHAT A SIGHT TO SEE

GOD, THE HOLY SPIRIT AND THEE

THE GARDENER AWAITS

ADAM'S SINS ARE

CLEANSED WITH BLOOD

JESUS DIED FOR YOU, TO BE

FREE OF DEATH FOR ETERNITY

OFF TO GALILEE

CHRIST IS RISEN

THE LORD IS GLORIFIED

ALLELUIA, ALLELUIA,

ALLELUIA

IN JESUS' NAME WE PRAY

2017

45

GOD

ROMANS, ACTS, JOHN, LUKE,
MARK, AND MATTHEW
YOUR EVERLASTING LOVE
IN YOUR NEW TESTAMENT
IN THE NAME OF JESUS
THE ORIGINAL SIN,
BROUGHT FORTH THE
DEATH OF HIM
YOUR SACRED HEART,
YOU SHATTERED DEATH
UPON THE CROSS
THE ETERNAL BREATH
MARY TIMES THREE
HOLY, HOLY, HOLY
TRINITY

PENTECOST
HOLY SPIRIT
RIGHTEOUS ONES
GENTILES HEAR IT
THE SCRIPTURES, REFLECT,
YOUR GRACE
AS WE LOOK ABOVE;
THE HUMAN RACE
ANGELIC VOICES, WE DO
RECALL, THEY CAME ALIGHT
THEY HEAR THE CALLS
ACCEPT MY SON, REDEEMING
FAITH, OPEN YOUR HEART
YOU'VE SEEN MY FACE

2017

EVENTUALLY

THE TREE OF LIFE
EVE, YOU KNEW WHERE TO STEP
THE SERPENT CAME AND
FULFILLED THE PLAN

DEATH TO THOSE, THOSE OF MAN
YOU SINNED, WE HEARD,
ADAM FOLLOWED SUIT.

GOD LOOKED, YOU WORE
A LEAF TO HIDE
THE SIN YOU TOOK, AND
HID YOUR PRIDE

YOU ATE THE FRUIT, YOU
LEARNED THE TRUTH,
HEAVEN FELL A BIT THAT DAY,
ADAM'S PROGENY WAS
CURSED YOU SAY.

IT ALL STARTED FROM
WHAT FELL, THE DEVIL WAS
BORN HE WENT TO HELL.

WHAT WE EAT, WE BECOME
THAT WHICH IS.
A SIN APART, THE WORK OF ART.
ADAM'S FLESH BECAME A SIN.

JESUS CAME BECAUSE OF HIM
HIS FLESH BECAME
WHAT WE NOW EAT,
TO REMEMBER, TO
BECOME HIM, AGAIN.

TO BE ONE WITH GOD, WE
RETURN TO TRUTH,
HEAVEN WANTS TO SEE YOU GROW,
LET GO OF SIN AND LOOK WITHIN,

YOU ARE PART OF GOD, WITH HIM.

A HYMN, A PRAYER, WE
RETURN TO GOD,
SAY YOU LOVE ME, AND NOD.

I LOVE YOU, LORD, GIVER OF LIFE.
I'M SORRY I SINNED, IT'S
BEHIND US, IT'S LIFE.

I EAT YOUR BREAD, AND
SHARE YOUR WINE,
I'M CLOSER TO GOD IT'S TIME.

AS YOU RAISE ME UP,
KNOW I'M FOUND.
I'M PART OF YOU, THE LAMB,
A CHRISTMAS GIFT APART.

THANK THE TREES, FOR
THE TIME WE'VE HAD,
THE LIGHT, THE TRUTH,
ETERNALLY.

WE RETURN TO YOU, FINALLY.
AMEN

2017

CHRIST SOCKS

AS I STITCH
I PRAY
OH, HOLY ONE
OUR LORD JESUS CHRIST
PLEASE GRANT ME THE STRENGTH
TO WALK IN YOUR WAYS
TO LIGHT THE EARTH WITH EACH STEP
AS I STITCH, I LOVE YOU MORE

I ASK YOU TO FILL ME WITH THE LIGHT OF CHRIST,
TO HEAR YOUR HEART SONG,
TO INTERTWINE YOUR LOVE IN MY STITCHES.
AMEN
MAY THE LIGHT OF JESUS CHRIST
EMERGE

2017

A TEAR FOR MY BELOVED

A DAY DEFINED BY LOSS
I LISTEN TO YOUR TEARS
HEAR MY CRY
MY HEART MOURNS FOR THEE
TAKE MY LOVE
AND LET IT SHINE
DOWN ON THEE
MY BELOVED
MY HUMANITY
I LOVE THEE
TAKE ME TO HEAVEN
TO INFINITY
ONLY A WHISPER
TO PETER I CRY
I SAY GOODBYE
DEVOTED TO JESUS

2017

SACRED HEART

LORD JESUS CHRIST
THE LIGHT
THE LOSS
I SEE
THE CROSS
GIVE INTO ME
SWEET JESUS
I BLEED
I NEED
YOUR LOVE
FROM UP
ABOVE
SWEET JESUS
THE WORDS
YOU SPEAK
RESONATE
WITH ME
YOUR HEART
IT KNOWS

ME
COMPLETELY
I SEE
YOU
SHINE
YOU ARE SO
MINE
THE
COMPLINE
ADORES
THEE
SWEET JESUS
THE CHRIST
WITHIN ME
LORD JESUS CHRIST
AMEN

PRIEST

HOLY SPIRIT	ME
LIGHT SURGER	EVANGELIST
PRAY FOR ME	PRAY
SWEET JESUS	RELIGIOUSLY
ANOMALY	SACRED
YOU ARE THE ONE	HEART
SHINE YOUR LIGHT	SAY MY NAME
HEAVENLY WORDS	GOD
SHINING BRIGHT	HEAVENLY FATHER
DOCTRINES	LORD
THEOLOGY	LITURGY
WORDS OF WISDOM	VESTMENT
EPIPHANY	FORGIVE
SUNDAY SCHOOL	ME
WORSHIP	I SERVE THEE
COVENANT	JESUS CHRIST
WITH	TRINITY

2016

IN LOVE U

```
        NU
     U      U
     N         U
  IN LOVE U
```

FEBRUARY 12, 2017

LOVE OF MY LIFE

WHEN I SEE YOUR CUTE SMILE
I RUN
TO
THE ONE
THAT I HOLD DEAR
I BRACE MYSELF
WHEN YOU ARE NEAR

I WANT YOU TO KNOW MY HEART
I'VE BEEN HERE FROM THE START
GOD WANTS US TO BE FRIENDS
NOTHING BETWEEN US, I
SAVED US ALREADY

WE ARE ETERNAL,
DON'T CHA KNOW
SO WE'RE TOGETHER,
IT'S ALL I KNOW

I LOVE YOU, SO MUCH
IT'S YOUR EYES, YOUR LIGHT
I CAN TELL
WE'LL BE ABLE TO OVERCOME HELL
HE'S NOT THAT STRONG
IN THE LIGHT
I'M SUPER, YOU'RE STRONG
LET'S LIGHT

BEING WITH YOU, FOREVER
I HEAR YOU SING, YOU'RE CLEVER
TOUCH MY HAND AGAIN,
I'M IN LOVE, YOUR AMEN

TEARS HAVE FALLEN
FROM MY EYES
WHEN YOU'RE NEAR, I'M ALL EYES
HUG AND KISS YOU, I'LL
ALWAYS MISS YOU

JESUS CHRIST, YOURS NOW,
THE STARS AND HEAVEN
LET'S BOW

MY HEART IS PART OF
YOURS, LET'S SHARE
YOU'RE MINE, JESUS LOVES IN KIND
TAKE ME OUT, AND
FIND TRUE LOVE,
I'M PART OF HEAVEN, UP ABOVE.
ANGELS TOAST, WHEN
THEY ARE SURE,

YOU'RE MINE TO LOVE,
IN KIND ENDURE.

I LOVE TO LOVE YOU
SHINE WITH ME,
HEAVEN'S BLESSING THANKFULLY.

LOVE OF MY LIFE, SEE YOU WITHIN,
MY HEART HEARS YOUR
VOICE, AGAIN AND AGAIN.

JESUS LOVES YOU AMEN!

NOVEMBER 11, 2016

EYES

OKAY
I CAN SEE WHY
YOUR KIDS CRY
WHEN THEY SEE
YOUR EYES
ONE GLANCE
ROMANCE
BEETHOVEN'S
DANCE
OPERA
WON'T STOP YA
UBC
WOULD GET
ON THEIR KNEES
TO HEAR YOU

GEEZ
HEAVEN WATCHES
YOUR EVERY MOVE
SPINDLING
TRANCED
I'M YOUR BRANCH
IT'S TIME
FOR YOUR RHYME

KISS ME
EYE SPY
MOSES KEEPS
A TAB ON YOU
LOVE YOUR NEIGHBOUR
AS HE LOVES YOU

2017

LOVELY PANTS, SWEATER

YOU ARE MY LIFE, IN THE WOMB
YOU APPEAR, I HOLD YOU NEAR
IN A CHANCE, WINTER ROMANCE
I HAVE A ROSE, THE NIGHT UNFOLDS
BABIES ARE HELD, I SEE YOU AND MELD
INTO YOUR HEART, LOOKING WITHIN
I AM COMPLETE, WITH YOU I GLEAM
A HUG FROM HERE, HEAVEN STEERS
THE NIGHT BEGINS, CHOCOLATE HEARTS
LEMON TARTS, UNDRESS,
I HOLD MY BREATH, LESS IS BEST
I CARESS..........

2018

JANUARY 31

YOUR EYES SING A TUNE
I LOOK UP AT THE MOON
STARS CRY OUT TO ME
GOD, JESUS, HOLY

STAY A WHILE
AND DANCE
ROMANTIC HAPPENSTANCE
BORN OF EASE AND LOVE
A SYMPHONY ABOVE
WINTERTIME PLAY
ICE, SNOW, SLATE
HEAVEN AWAITS

HALOS RING
ALLELUIAS SING
GLORY TO THEE
MOST HOLY
TO BE A QUEEN

OF HEARTS
TO SERVE
WITH LOVE
YOU'RE STRONG
THAT'S WHY
WE BELONG

SING TO ME
LOOK AT MY EYES
YOU WONDER
YOU'RE WISE

I SEE YOU
INSIDE
YOU'RE NEW

SPIRITUAL LOVE
WIDE AWAKE
ENLIGHTEN US

FLY AWAY

AIR DOES MOVE
IT'S QUARTER TO TWO
VENUS IS READY
THE ROSE IS TOO
THE KING
ABOVE
HEAVEN'S TOUCH
YOU KNOW SO MUCH
NINE OF CLUBS
JOHN 12:1-3

ANOINTED WITH LOVE
AT BETHANY
SIX OF DIAMONDS
KARMIC WALK
ALL JUPITER
EXPANSIVE GLOW
BLESSINGS
I'M JESUS
YOU KNOW
I'LL GIVE YOU LIFE
ACTS 2:32
GOD IN LOVE WITH YOU

APRIL 27, 2017 4:00 P.M.

EB HAIKU

ELOQUENT BASHFUL
TIMELESS BEAUTY IN THE LIGHT
HER FIGURE, HOURGLASS

2018

GRACE

I SEE YOU WALK BY
IT'S IN YOUR EYES
THE ASTONISHING
GRACE
THE WAY YOU MOVE
YOUR HANDS
THE HONOUR
IN BOWING
THE KISS
YOUR HAIR
YOU KNOW
I CARE
YOUR EASY SMILE

THE KNOWING
GLANCE
IT'S IN YOUR VOICE
HEAVEN IS WISE
TO HAVE CHOSEN
YOU
I DELIGHT
IN SEEING
YOUR
GRACE
A GIFT
THANKS BE TO
GOD

2017

CONFESSION

WE SPEAK IN RHYMES
UNTIL IT'S TIME FOR
CONFESSION
WE PLAY THE PART
IT'S TRULY ART
I LOVE YOU
NAKED
WE STAND
HAND IN HAND
BLESSINGS
JESUS IS THERE
HE KNOWS
WE CARE

WE LOVE HIM
WE PRAY
ON OUR KNEES
GOD HEARS
OUR
PLEAS
ALLELUIA

THE ART OF LOVE, AND THE
PERMISSION WE GIVE TO THOSE
IN LOVE AND LIGHT TO HEAR US.
AMEN

NOVEMBER 25, 2016

THE VOW

TRUE LOVE IS AN ART FORM
WHEN WE BECOME THAT WHICH IS

LIGHT WILL SHINE FROM WITHIN

TAKE MY HAND
WALK WITH ME
SAY A PRAYER
MINE IN HEAVEN
HERE ON EARTH
FLY LIKE A PHOENIX
LIGHT UP THE WIND

I'M HERE TO BE
THE WORD OF GOD
ETERNALLY

APRIL 13, 2017

LIGHT

HEART SONG   SACRAMENT

HEAR MY VOICE   INFINITY

TOUCH MY HEART   ONENESS

SING TO ME   HEAVEN'S ANGELS

BREATHE INTO EXISTENCE   BETHLEHEM

LIGHT UP MY LIFE   STAR SHINE

SMILE   BE MINE

ETERNALLY   JOHN 1

YOURS   WITNESS

JESUS   LIFE

LORD'S PRAYER

BREAD OF LIFE   AMEN

LAMB OF GOD

2016

SACRED SOUL

LOVERS LIGHT

SAY A PRAYER

TOUCH MY HEART

SING MY PART

HAVE A SONG

SING ALONG

LAVENDER

CHERRY BLOSSOM

PETALS

STREAMING

RAIN

DROPS

GLEAMING

REMINISCE

SHARE THE LIGHT

READ A POEM

CANDLELIGHT

JESUS LOVES ME

GO TO CHURCH

MOTHER MARY

IN LOVE WITH YOU

PLEASING HEART

GIVING LIGHT

FOREVER YOURS

IN WHITE

2016

MY HEART IS YOURS

UNTIL THIS DAY

I HAD NOT REALIZED

THE LOVE

THAT I FOUND

FROM THIS DAY FORWARD

I DIE TO YOU

FROM THIS DAY ON

I REMEMBER.....

WE ARE INTERTWINED

LIKE THE TREES AND THE WIND

GO FORTH IN LOVE

MY HEART BEATS

THE RHYTHM OF YOUR LOVE

MY HEART IS YOURS

FROM THIS DAY ON

WE ARE ONE

MARCH 10, 2015 10:31 P.M.

LOVELY

SITTING BY MY SIDE, INSIDE MY HEART
THROB, US TOGETHER, US INTERTWINED
LEAVES US, DELIGHTED, CANDLES LIT
SMALL EXCHANGES, GLANCES, WITHIN,
MY SENSES, MASTER ME, TONIGHT, WE
SING, DUETS, IN LOVE, FEEL ME, MY LOVE
MARRY ME, MAGNIFICENT ONE.

IN GOD WE TRUST
VERILY, VERILY IN LOVE AMEN

FEBRUARY 12, 2017

HEART IN SOUL

I FEEL YOUR WAVES, ENTER MY HEART, THE PASSION UNFOLDS.
MOON LIGHT, WATER'S EDGE, SAY A PRAYER, I'M SAID.
THE WORD OF GOD LIES WITHIN, STREAMS OF LIGHT
HEAVEN GLISTENS, BE STILL MY HEART, BLOSSOMS FALL
THE MOMENT WE UNITE.
LIE AWAKE, KNOW MY LIGHT, HEAVEN'S WAY UP, I'M BESIDES.
YOU REACH IN AND HOLD YOUR OWN, I'M BEAUTY UNKNOWN.

STARS HOLD THE TIMELESS REFLECTION, WAVES APART, INFLECTION.
JUPITER SOUNDING LIGHT, ROLLING THUNDER UPRIGHT.
I HOLD YOUR HAND, THE SAND IT KNOWS I AM.

LOVING YOU, WITHIN FOREVER
JESUS LOVES YOU
TONIGHT

NOVEMBER 7, 2016

ANGEL

ANGELIC	LOYALTY
AMEN	FLIGHT
HALLELUJAH	SERAPHIM
WHISPER	CHERUBIM
FLIGHT	HOLY
AERODYNAMIC	SERVE THE LORD
WHITE	RESONANCE
HALO	SWOOSH
CHILDREN OF GOD	HEAR MY PRAYER
PERFECTION	LORD
UNITED	IN THE NAME OF JESUS
LUMINOUS	CHRIST
FLY	BOW
WINGS	CHURCH
HELD IN PRAYER	CHAPEL
EUCHARIST	CROSS
HONOUR	AMEN

2016

THE VOICE OF AN ANGEL

IS THAT HEAVEN I SEE

THE ANGELS ARE

BRINGING DOWN THEE

"THE VOICE OF AN ANGEL"

SHE BRINGS THE LIGHT

I HEAR THE SONG OF HER SOUL

SHE SINGS SOLO

I KNOW WHY I AM HERE

TO BE WITH HER

WHEN TWO BECOME ONE

LIKE THE MOON AND THE SUN

A SHARED DREAM

A LOVE SONG

WHEN TWO BECOME ONE

LA DA DE BECOME ONE WITH ME

YOU SHOULD HEAR THE SOUND

OF HER VOICE, THE SONG OF LOVE

INFUSES MY SOUL

I LOVE THEE

LIKE HEAVEN AND THE TREES

BECOME ONE WITH ME

MY LOVELY

SPRING 2015

STILLNESS

THE WAVES
THEY ASPIRE
TO BE LIKE YOU,
PERFECTLY CLEAR,
PERFECTLY NEW
MOON RELEASE ME
FROM THIS TIDE
AS I LOOK INTO YOUR EYES
THE REFLECTION
IS MINE

THE SAND IT SHOWS
MY FOOTPRINT
I'M READY
TO STAND
I'LL ALWAYS

BE
I AM

STILLNESS APART
GRAVITATIONAL PULL
EMOTIONAL MOMENT
I'M FULL
VENUS UNITE

STARS SHINE
JUPITER'S GLOW
HEAVEN ALREADY KNOWS
MARY SHE'S ONE
IN LOVE WITH JESUS
THE SON

2017

EBB AND FLOW

WE EBB AND WE FLOW, AS WE WATCH THE
LIGHT GROW.
INTO YOUR HEART, STREAMS OF PASSION,
WE KISS, I FALL INTO YOUR EMBRACE, MY
HEART ABLAZE.
INTO THE LIGHT, JUST RIGHT.
YOU COME UNDONE, WE ARE ONE, THE
STARTS DO SHINE, THE MOON UNITES THE LIGHT.
THE WATER MARKS THE TIDE, REFLECTED
MOON LIGHT, WAVE CRESTS, UNDULATING
THIGHS.

2017

SEVEN SONG

IS IT ABOUT MY MUSCLES, WELL IT'S ABOUT MY HEART...
WHEN I LOOK IN THE MIRROR IT'S A START
HOW DID I GET HERE, WHO DO I BECOME
THE HOLIEST OH HOLY...OR A NUN

A PRIEST, IT'S MY PLAN, I KNEW FROM THE START, I'M STARING INTO
AN OCEAN, WHERE DO WE PART. IF ONLY I HAD MOSES' COURAGE TO
TAKE YOU THROUGH THE SEA, OR JESUS' MINISTRY WE ARE GODS
CHILDREN, I'M SEVEN, IN THE FLESH, LOVE STANDS STILL IF YOU LET
LOVE INTO YOUR HEART. IT SEARCHES TO FIND YOU IN THE DARK.

DON'T STOP SEARCHING TO FIND THE ONE, YOU
WILL SOON REALIZE IT IS GODS SON.
I'M READY NOW, JESUS, I'VE COME TO THIS PART, I'M HOLY, I'M ART.

Printed in the United States
By Bookmasters